Ranger Trails

Jobs of Adventure in America's Parks

Lori Yanuchi

Jeff Yanuchi

Illustrated by James R. Morris

Ridge Rock Press
Healy, Alaska

Ranger Trails: Jobs of Adventure in America's Parks

All rights reserved.

Copyright 2005 by Lori Yanuchi, Jeff Yanuchi, and Gina Soltis.

Artwork copyright 2005 James R. Morris.

This is a work of fiction. The names, characters, and incidents depicted in this book are the product of the authors' imagination or are used fictitiously. Any resemblance to actual persons is coincidental.

The web sites listed in this book are for reference purposes only and are not endorsed by the writers, artist or publisher.

Editor: Gina Soltis

Library of Congress Control Number 2005902435

ISBN 0-9670177-2-6

Ridge Rock Press
SAN #253-6595
P.O. Box 255
Healy, Alaska 99743

Printed in the United States of America

For all kids thinking of a career in conservation: follow your heart, and your dreams will come true!
Lori Yanuchi

To all seasonal park rangers, the backbone of the Service.
Jeff Yanuchi

To my parents, Richard and Judy, who raised me to appreciate the world around me and to my wife, Jennie-also known as "Sunshine"-for encouraging me to share my gift.
James R. Morris

Table of Contents

Meet the Rangers	1
Grand Canyon National Park	2
Dinosaur National Monument	6
Mesa Verde National Park	8
Independence National Historic Park	10
Hawaii Volcanoes National Park	12
Crater Lake National Park	14
Mount Rainier National Park	16
Acadia National Park	18
Gates of the Arctic National Park	22
Yellowstone National Park	24
Everglades National Park	28
Cape Hatteras National Seashore	32
Glacier National Park	34
Yosemite National Park	38
Denali National Park	40
Ranger History	44
Work in America's Parks	45
Volunteers	46
Man and the Biosphere	47
Ranger Skills	48
Web Sites	50
Glossary	54
Suggested Reading	57

Meet the Rangers

America's parks—they belong to all of us. National parks, state parks, county and city parks—all exist for us to enjoy the best of America. From desert to mountain, ocean to prairie, from reenactment of Colonial times to present day music concerts, our parks tell the story of America, its land and its people.

What is cooler than America's parks? The people who work in them! Wherever you go - the city, the mountains, the desert or the ocean - there is a national park near you! In each park there are secrets for you to find and treasures for you to explore. You have a lot of discovering to do since there are over 380 places where rangers work. In each and every park, there is someone who will help you unlock the mystery and open the door to discovery. This person has the most awesome job of all—Park Ranger!

Rangers answer questions and give programs.
Rangers make the parks safe.
Rangers study the animals, the land, and the history.
Rangers have the coolest jobs on the planet!

Turn the pages and find out why!

Your Search for Adventure Follows . . .

Web sites: There are over 250 web sites listed in this book! Look for web sites in each of the park stories and in the list in the back of the book. To quickly link to all of these sites, go to www.rangertrailsadventure.com.

Critical issues: Can Karelian bear dogs help save grizzly bears? How does water flow through the Grand Canyon affect fishing in the Gulf of California? Will the gray wolf be taken off the endangered species list? Find out about these critical issues and others that park rangers face today. Like a stone in a pond, decisions made in our parks ripple over boundary lines, affecting a web of surrounding ecosystems. Find *"The Big Picture"* section of each story to learn how you can help protect America's parks and the ecological webs surrounding them, and then get involved!

Words in green print: In the stories, words appearing in green print can be found in the glossary, in the back of this book.

Symbols: When you see the following symbols throughout the book, it means that park has special importance to the world, designated by the United Nations Man and the Biosphere Program:

 International Biosphere Reserve

 Wetland of International Significance

 World Heritage Site

To learn more about these special places, go to the Man and the Biosphere section in the back of the book.

A raft disappears behind a wall of whitewater, while the sound of the river booms through the canyon like thunder.

"Whoa," thinks Jason, "this is some gnarly water!"

Jason is with his family on a beach in the Grand Canyon. The Colorado River is rushing by them only a few feet away. Upstream, the raft crests a wave like it was on the back of a bronco.

Jason yells to his sister, "Yo, they're going to lose it!"

The two people in the raft scramble around, straining at the oars. They round a rock outcrop and fight their way to an eddy by Jason's beach.

The Big Picture...

Colorado...mighty river?

Do you know the Colorado River is 1,450 miles long and flows into the Pacific Ocean? But not before thirsty cities and farms in the Southwest United States and Mexico take what they need. Eleven dams and canals on the Colorado **divert** precious water to over 25 million people who depend on it. The mighty Colorado is reduced to a trickle by the time it reaches its delta in Mexico at the Gulf of California.

Learn more at **www.water-ed.org** or **www.nps.gov/grca**.

When the raft hits the beach, the two people in the raft give each other high fives. "Yeah man, we did it!" "Woowee, that was sweet!"

Jason looks at them and then at the big raft. "I didn't think you were going to make it!."

"Hey, we're trained professionals," grins one. "Plus," he says, pointing to a patch on his life vest, "we are park rangers."

"Cool," Jason thinks, "very cool." "So, what do you do?" he asks.

"Well . . . we seek out the worst water and . . . " the other ranger punches him in the arm. "Well," says the first ranger, "what we *really* do is patrol the river. We talk to river users, help people who are injured or having problems with their boat; even rescue people if we need to." His partner adds, "We also make sure boaters follow the rules we have to protect the river. Still, the best part of the job is running the rapids!"

"Man, I want to be a ranger and run the river!" Jason could barely keep from yelling.

Look in the back of this book to find out how Jason might become a ranger!

Riverbanks and canyon walls are windows in time, great places to look for fossils. There are other places that hold the secrets of fossils too . . .

The Big Picture . . .

Dam It!

Glen Canyon Dam and Hoover Dam control the water flow through Grand Canyon National Park. Park managers are struggling to understand the long-term effects these dams have on river and riparian ecology. Many miles downstream at the mouth of the Colorado the delta ecosystem has collapsed. The nutrient rich alluvium that once fed one of the richest estuaries in the world is absent.

What can be done to help the Colorado River? Check out www.americanrivers.org or www.nps.gov/glca or www.usbr.gov/lc/hooverdam.

Katie's dream has come true - she and her family are camping in Dinosaur National Monument! Today they are at the quarry watching a team of National Park Service paleontologists digging around a newly found allosaurus fossil. Katie loves all dinosaurs, but the big hunters are her favorite.

Katie replays last night's hunt in her mind. The allosaurus, its razor sharp teeth hungry to bite into some meat, stalked its prey. Through the brush the mighty hunter silently roamed. It caught the scent of . . . hot dogs! "Mom, Katie is stealing a hot dog from the grill," her little brother Steve had whined, putting an end to her game.

But now here at the quarry, one of the paleontologists from the dig is walking over to them! That snaps Katie back to the present day!

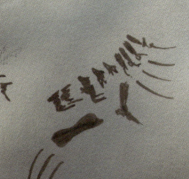

Ranger Bernadette tells Katie "By studying bones we can learn a lot about dinos, like what they ate, how they raised their young, and how they died. When I was your age, Katie, I really dug old bones too"! This is music to Katie's ears!

The allosaurus senses different prey, close by and begins to chase. The six-year-old boy is too slow . . . "Mom . . . !"

What would you like to be when you grow up?

Fossils help us study the history of the natural world, but there are parks where rangers study ancient humans too . . .

The Big Picture . . .

Road wars?

Many national parks in the western United States and Alaska are facing new threats from an old law. The Mining Act of 1866 known as RS2477 allows for the construction of highways on public lands. Some state and local governments claim that horse, cattle, hiking and jeep trails used before parks were established should be turned into roads that would crisscross proposed wilderness areas. Learn more about RS2477 and what you can do to help at www.RS2477.com or www.nps.gov/dino.

As a class project, Mrs. Wolfe's students are researching ancient civilizations on the Internet. Aaron chose to do his report on the Anasazi culture.

During Aaron's research he discovers that these people lived in the American Southwest over 1,000 years ago. Archeologists use picks, shovels, brushes and maps to learn how these people lived. Aaron uses a computer, printer and a modem to visit several National Park Service web sites to get his information.

He finds out that the Anasazi people were primarily cliff dwellers. They built their villages in the natural alcoves found in the steep sandstone canyons and made ladders to access the rim and tend their crops. After visiting many web sites, Aaron is excited to learn that no one really knew what had happened to all the people! Aaron really loves mysteries, and this is a big one! Why would thousands of people leave their homes and disappear?

Aaron e-mails an archeologist park ranger at Mesa Verde National Park to find out more. She responds, "We used to think it was because of a war, but our digs show no evidence that this is true. More likely it may have been a lack of food caused by drought, poor crops or overhunting. But the truth is, these are just our best guesses, and what really happened to the Anasazi people will probably remain an unsolved mystery."

What do you think happened to the Anasazi?

Human history in our parklands goes back a long time. The Anasazi were here thousands of years before America's parks were born. Some parks celebrate the birth of our country . . .

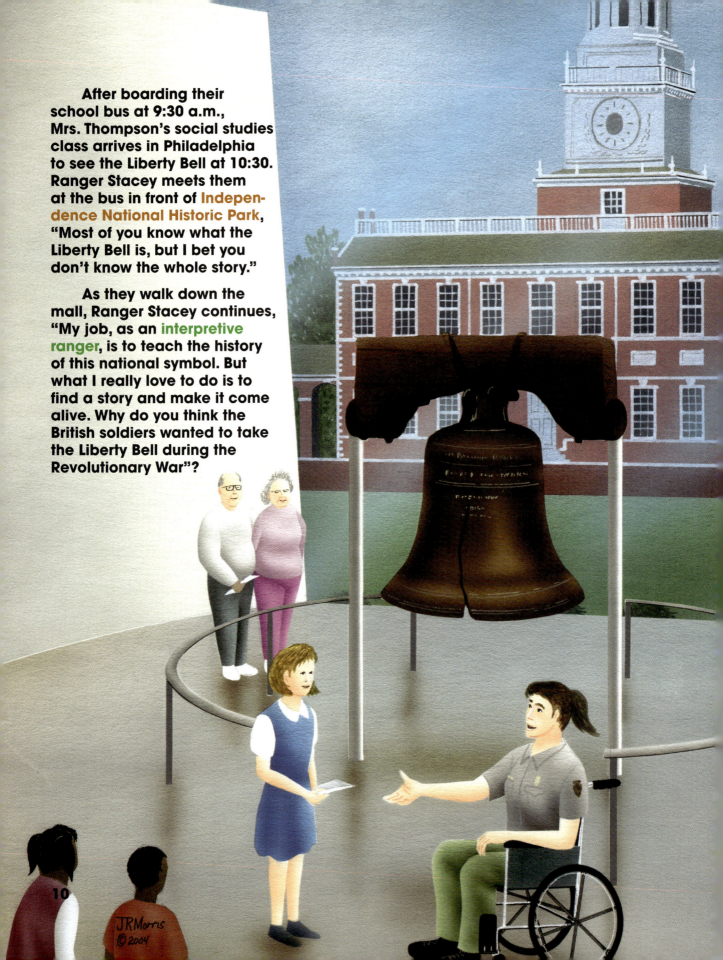

After boarding their school bus at 9:30 a.m., Mrs. Thompson's social studies class arrives in Philadelphia to see the Liberty Bell at 10:30. Ranger Stacey meets them at the bus in front of **Independence National Historic Park**, "Most of you know what the Liberty Bell is, but I bet you don't know the whole story."

As they walk down the mall, Ranger Stacey continues, "My job, as an *interpretive ranger*, is to teach the history of this national symbol. But what I really love to do is to find a story and make it come alive. Why do you think the British soldiers wanted to take the Liberty Bell during the Revolutionary War"?

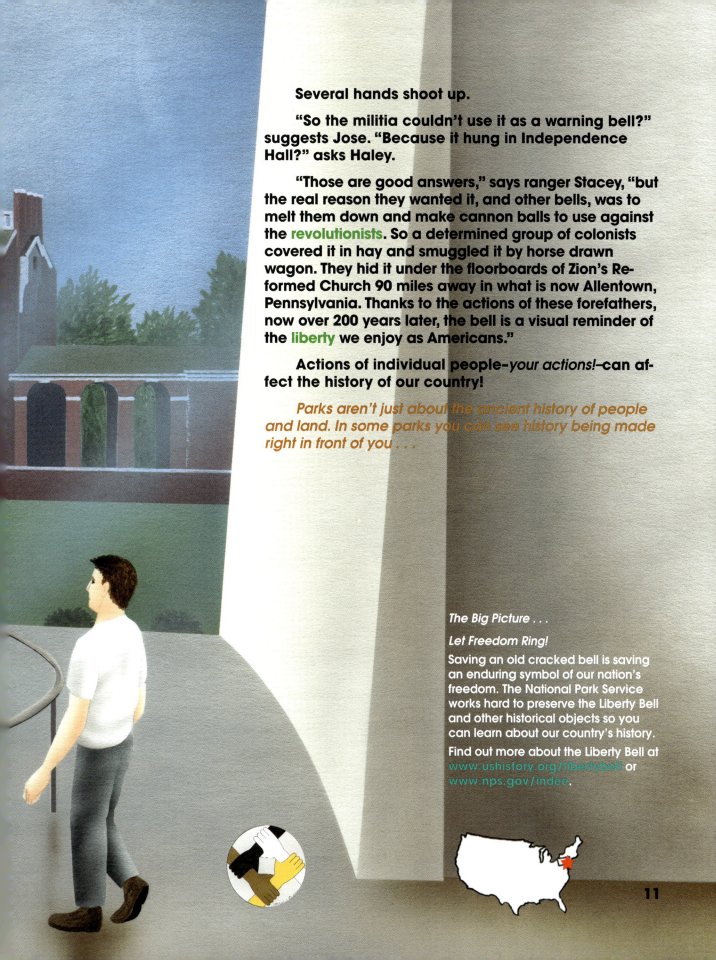

Several hands shoot up.

"So the militia couldn't use it as a warning bell?" suggests Jose. "Because it hung in Independence Hall?" asks Haley.

"Those are good answers," says ranger Stacey, "but the real reason they wanted it, and other bells, was to melt them down and make cannon balls to use against the revolutionists. So a determined group of colonists covered it in hay and smuggled it by horse drawn wagon. They hid it under the floorboards of Zion's Reformed Church 90 miles away in what is now Allentown, Pennsylvania. Thanks to the actions of these forefathers, now over 200 years later, the bell is a visual reminder of the liberty we enjoy as Americans."

Actions of individual people–*your actions!*–can affect the history of our country!

Parks aren't just about the ancient history of people and land. In some parks you can see history being made right in front of you . . .

The Big Picture . . .

Let Freedom Ring!

Saving an old cracked bell is saving an enduring symbol of our nation's freedom. The National Park Service works hard to preserve the Liberty Bell and other historical objects so you can learn about our country's history.

Find out more about the Liberty Bell at www.ushistory.org/libertybell or www.nps.gov/indee.

"Pele', the goddess of creation and destruction, has lived in the volcano since the beginning of time," says Ranger Jay during his program at Hawaii Volcanoes National Park. "When you walk on the trails in the park you will be able to see Pele's tears and hair."

After hearing the program, Vijay and his dad are careful to stay on the marked trail because Ranger Jay said that walking on lava formations could be tricky and dangerous. During their walk, they meet the park vulcanologist, Ranger Alaha, who tells them "Lava comes from the earth's core which lies miles below the earth's surface! The lava is really rock that is so hot it became liquid. When it cools, it makes all kinds of wild formations. Some of these wild formations are what we native Hawaiians call Pele's tears and Pele's hair."

Vijay and his dad then walk to Apua Point where they watch the red hot lava flow into the sea. Steam is everywhere, and the colors are intense. "This," says his dad, "is how new land is formed!"

Vijay thinks, "Vulcanologists have a hot job!"

Do you know where there are other volcanoes in the United States?

Some volcanoes are active, and some aren't. America's parks let you see both . . .

The Big Picture . . .

Invasion!

What do insects, snakes, pigs and weeds have in common? All are exotic species invading the Hawaii Volcanoes ecosystem. Why is this bad? They destroy habitat, steal food and crowd out many endangered plants and animals found only in Hawaii.

Find out what can be done to stop the invasion at www.hear.org or www.nps.gov/havo

The weather has been hot and dry all summer. Jose and his family are on vacation for two weeks, driving up the coastline from Los Angeles, California to Oregon. As they pull into the Cloudcap Overlook, Jose was excited to see Crater Lake National Park. Parked at the edge of the lot was a gleaming white and red fire truck, with six wildland firefighters.

"This is awesome, just like the firefighters I saw on TV!" Jose runs over to the fire crew. "Hey, are you fighting wildfires?" "Yes", the closest one answers, "we're part of Crater Lake's fire crew." "What are you doing *here*?" Looking at the pullout, Jose doesn't see many trees around.

"We are preparing an area in the forest north of here in case it burns. We are digging a fireline and cutting down hazard trees, which are what you call dead trees." "With chain saws, right?" "Right." "Then why are you *here*?" repeats Jose. "A lot of lightning was seen in a big thunderstorm around here a half hour ago, so we're staging here in case there are more lightning strikes."

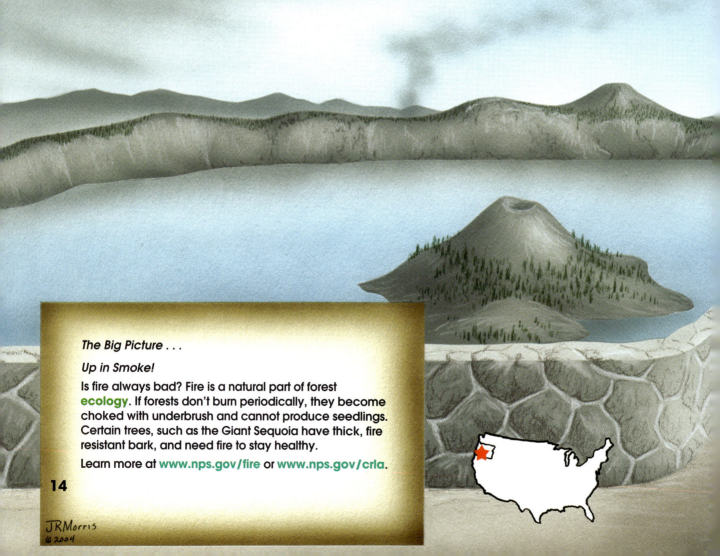

The Big Picture . . .

Up in Smoke!

Is fire always bad? Fire is a natural part of forest ecology. If forests don't burn periodically, they become choked with underbrush and cannot produce seedlings. Certain trees, such as the Giant Sequoia have thick, fire resistant bark, and need fire to stay healthy.

Learn more at www.nps.gov/fire or www.nps.gov/crla.

Just then, a loud tone comes over the radio. "Lisa, we need to go!" yells one of the other fire crew members. "Smoke reported near Oasis Butte!" "Gotta go!" Lisa tells Jose. "Be careful!" Jose waves as the engine pulls away with lights flashing.

"Wow" says Jose, "*real heroes*, just like on TV! Meeting them *made* my vacation!"

Can forest fires ever be a good thing?

The mountains made by volcanoes can be the best place to look for adventure in America's parks . . .

Excitement is high among the group of kids at the Paradise Visitor Center.

"This is going to be so cool!" David had always wanted to be a mountain climber. Now, he and the rest of the group are meeting real mountaineering rangers right here in Mount Rainier National Park.

Rangers Dan and Nicole are surrounded by a mountain of neatly displayed gear and equipment. Tents, climbing ropes, harnesses, ice axes, carabiners–everything a ranger would need for a successful patrol on the top of a large, glacier covered volcano.

The kids gather around the gear. "How do you carry all that stuff? It looks heavy." "Why do you need parkas up there in the summer?" "Is there a rope all the way to the top?" "Did you ever have to rescue anybody?"

Rangers Dan and Nicole patiently answer all the questions. "The gear looks heavier than it is and is easy to carry when packed carefully into backpacks. On snow, at 14,000 feet in elevation, it is cold even in summer. No, there isn't a rope to the top, and yes, sometimes we have to rescue people." The rangers talk about the two most important factors of a successful climb: preparation and safety.

Ranger Dan asks if any of the kids wanted to be a mountaineering ranger. David's hand shoots up faster than anyone's. Ranger Nicole smiles, "Hey, we have quite an eager volunteer! What's your name?" "It's 'David,' and I want to climb mountains!" "Excellent! Let's see what it's like when we put the gear on you."

For the next twenty minutes the rangers dress David in climbing gear, starting out with a windproof hat and headlamp on his head, and ending up with crampons on his feet. The rangers show the group how to use an ice ax and how to tie knots needed for alpine climbing.

Ranger Nicole asks David, "Well, do you still want to be a mountaineering ranger?" "You bet, I'm ready to climb tomorrow!"

They all laugh, and David knows that one day he would be back with all his own climbing gear, ready to reach the top of Mt. Rainier!

The Big Picture . . .

Tread Lightly

Colonies of tiny lichens, mosses and wildflowers growing on rocky slopes . . . pikas, marmots and wild sheep . . . how is it possible for mountains to sustain such life? The alpine ecosystem is perfectly adapted to life above the treeline and is very delicate. Tread lightly!

Find out more at www.Lnt.org or www.nps.gov/mora.

Some rangers use ice axes and crampons to patrol their parks, while others use more familiar equipment . . .

"242, Park Dispatch." The call comes over the radio from park headquarters in Acadia National Park.

"This is 242, go ahead", Ranger Shay answers. "We have a report of an injured bicyclist near the Thunder Hole pullout."

Ranger Shay responds to the scene with the emergency lights on his ranger patrol vehicle flashing. He sees a little boy sitting on the bike trail holding his arm. His bicycle is lying askew beside him. The grown ups with him look worried.

A woman approaches Ranger Shay as soon as he steps out of his truck. "I'm Julia", she says excitedly. "My son Parker was riding way too fast around a corner . . . I yelled for him to slow down, but it was too late . . . he lost control and fell off his bike . . . I'm afraid his arm is broken!" "I'll go check him out Julia," Ranger Shay says with calm reassurance as he gathers his emergency bag and walks over.

The Big Picture . . .

Clear the Air

Smog, gridlock, overcrowding - these are not things that typically come to mind when we think of America's parks. How do you squeeze over 4 million visitors per year into the fifth smallest national park?

Think propane fueled shuttle buses . . .

"Hi Parker, I'm Shay, your mom said you took a spill and hurt your arm."

"She's really mad at me, if it's busted she's gonna kill me!" Parker moans.

"Let's take a look at it. Do you hurt any place else?" asks Shay. "No", replies Parker. "Well, at least you were wearing a safety helmet. That protected your head," Shay says as he conducts an initial assessment. He then begins to clean and bandage Parker's arm. "I think you're safe with your mom. Your arm is scraped pretty badly, but there's no swelling".

Ranger Shay turns to the family, "I don't think it's broken, but you should have a doctor take a look at it and have the bandages changed."

Parker asks, "Your ranger truck is cool, does it have a siren?" "Yep, want to hear it?" "Sure!"

Looking at all the police gear inside the truck Parker asks, "what's all this for?" "In case I have to catch bad guys," smiles Ranger Shay. "Do you ever?!" "Sometimes, but mostly I make sure people do the speed limit while they're driving in the park, but as a Law Enforcement Ranger, I have to be prepared for anything," Shay tells him. "Awesome!" whispers Parker. "Funny, I don't think his arm hurts anymore," his mother says smiling.

"This is 242 clear of accident scene," Shay speaks into his radio. CRACKLE! "Copy 242, report of an RV broken down near Cadillac Mountain entrance and blocking traffic," came the reply from dispatch. "242 responding," says Shay.

"Enjoy the park folks, and Parker . . . keep your bike on the trail!" "Darn, I wanted to hear more about catching bad guys!" says Parker.

A patrol vehicle is a pretty cool way to get around, but there is another way that lets a ranger cover more ground . . .

The Big Picture . . .

Clear the Air, part 2

Since use of propane powered shuttle buses began in 1999, Acadia has over 88,000 less cars on the park road and over 33% fewer emissions in the air. There are over 100 types of alternative transportation systems being used in many different national parks. Can you think of some other examples?

Check it out at www.nsp.gov/acad or www.nps.gov/transportation.

"Look over there to the west! I see them!"

The sun glints off the airplane's window as Ranger Pete maneuvers the Super Cub towards the herd of caribou. Ranger Pete is a park pilot for Gates of the Arctic National Park and Preserve in Alaska. His passenger, sitting behind him in the small, two-seat plane is Ranger Emily, a biologist counting the number of calves in a large herd of caribou. As park pilot, Ranger Pete goes to many locations. Sometimes, like today, he flies with biologists studying wildlife. Sometimes he drops off backcountry

rangers to remote camps. Sometimes he flies along the park boundary looking for poachers. His favorite job is to fly to bush villages and talk to natives who have lived a subsistence lifestyle for many generations.

"136, 137, 138 . . . that's all I see." Emily smiles. She is pleased that there are more calves now than at this time last year. The caribou herd is doing well despite a severe winter. Emily knows that now she can make 12 year old Jacky happy too. Jacky had read about the bad weather in the newspaper, and had sent a letter to the park asking if the caribou were OK. Emily would reply to him tonight.

Ranger Pete smiles too. He is doing what he loved to do best, flying over the wilderness of Alaska as a park ranger!

Can you think of other things a ranger pilot might do?

Caribou are the foundation of the arctic food chain. They have provided food and clothing to people for thousands of years, but they are just as important to natural predators . . . like wolves . . .

The Big Picture . . .

Bush Living

For countless generations, native people of the far north have used what the land and water provide: whale, beaver, salmon, caribou, berries and other wild plants and animals. Climate change has begun to affect this harsh but fragile environment. For the thousands of Alaskans living in the bush, where there are no roads and no malls, the natural resources they use from their ancestral land are now threatened.

Learn more at www.nativeknowledge.org or www.nps.gov/gaar.

Aaaawwoooo!! It seemed to come from everywhere.

Lee and Hannah look at each other. "Wow! What was that?!"

"That," says Mom, "is the howl of wolves."

"Cool!" Lee and Hannah yell at the same time. "Do you think we'll ever see them?" During their week long camping trip with their parents in Yellowstone National Park, Lee and Hannah had enjoyed encountering many of the park's animal inhabitants. The

The Big Picture . . .

The Howling

After a silence of nearly fifty years, the howling of wolves has returned to Yellowstone National Park. Recovery efforts began in 1995 when fourteen wolves were released in the park. Reintroduction has been so successful it has exceeded the goal of about one hundred wolves. The balance between predator and prey is once again complete in America's first national park.

Run with the wolf packs of Yellowstone at www.nps.gov/yell.

four had just returned from their afternoon hike and were a quarter mile from camp. The sun was setting when the call of the wolves pierced the twilight.

"Sssh!" Dad whispers, "look over there!" He points to a spot a short distance away where the trail crossed a small meadow.

One . . . two . . . three . . . four . . . five shadows emerge from the trees. They silently cross the meadow in single file, then melt into the darkness on the other side. Wolves!

Lee and Hannah are so excited they barely sleep that night. At daybreak they return to the meadow to look for sign of the wolves. Their efforts are rewarded with several distinct tracks in the mud. While Hannah makes casts of the tracks with plaster kits they had brought with them, Lee finds a small tuft of gray fur in the brush and some scat further away.

Later that night, the whole family hikes to a campground program given by a park ranger. Ranger Jim says, "One of the signs of a healthy ecosystem is having a balance between predators and prey. There are all kinds of predators in Yellowstone National Park. Robins eat worms, hawks and owls eat small birds and animals, fox and lynx eat hares, and grizzly and wolves eat deer, elk, and sometimes bison. Has anyone here seen any of Yellowstone's predators?"

Hannah and Lee's hands shoot up like a geyser.

"What did you see?" asks Jim. "We saw wolves!" they shout in unison, still excited by last night's encounter. "Oh," smiles Ranger Jim, "tell us about it!"

They tell their tale of adventure and show the casts they made. Ranger Jim says, "People use the wolf to symbolize many different things, but I think the most important thing about Canis lupus in Yellowstone is just that they are here."

"So do we," say Hannah and Lee, "So do we!"

Do you know of other places in the United States where the gray wolf lives?

Yellowstone is a park high in the mountains. Most of it is over one mile in elevation. Yet in other parks you might not get even 20 feet above sea level . . .

The Big Picture . . .

The Howling part 2

Wolf populations are so strong in the western states that the gray wolf has been down listed from an endangered, to a threatened species designation in most of the lower 48 states. The U.S. Fish and Wildlife Service will now begin the process to delist the gray wolf from the Endangered Species Act. States must first have a plan in place to ensure sustainable populations.

Voice your opinion at www.fws.gov.

Five minutes into their hike on the Everglades National Park Anhinga Trail boardwalk, Maria and the rest of Miss Pierre's class stop in their tracks.

"Check it out!" Hector is excited. "It's a crocodile, like on that TV show!" "Crikey! No way!" laughs Maria, "It's an alligator." "Oh yeah, how do you know?" huffs Hector.

"Cause it's in fresh water, has a rounded nose, not pointy, and it's black," says Maria triumphantly. "Well Maria, looks like you were paying attention this morning," Ranger Isabel has been with Miss Pierre's class all day and would be all week.

"Hey, I was too!" says Hector, "I know the Everglades is really a river, and that the canals and levees and pollution have been tough for the glades." "Very good Hector," Ranger Isabel looks at the class, "We all need to pay attention to the Everglades. After all, it's where our water comes from. Tomorrow, you won't just see the glades, you'll feel it!"

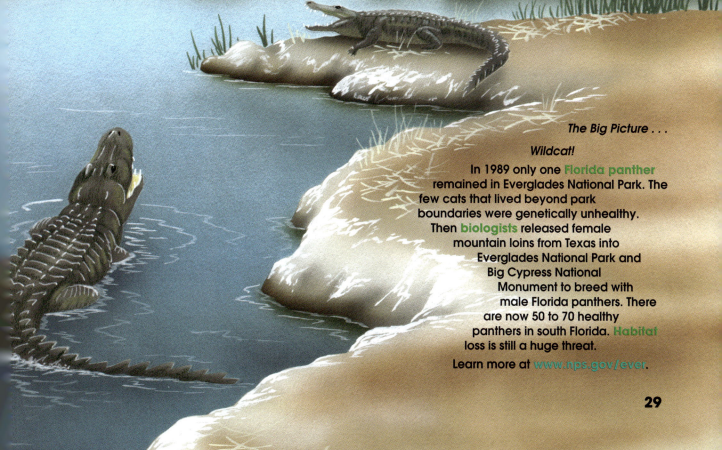

The Big Picture . . .

Wildcat!

In 1989 only one Florida panther remained in Everglades National Park. The few cats that lived beyond park boundaries were genetically unhealthy. Then biologists released female mountain loins from Texas into Everglades National Park and Big Cypress National Monument to breed with male Florida panthers. There are now 50 to 70 healthy panthers in south Florida. Habitat loss is still a huge threat.

Learn more at www.nps.gov/ever.

By 10:00 a.m. the next day, the class is up to their knees in a slough of the Everglades. Everyone is looking in Maria's net. "What is it?" someone asks.

"It looks like a baby lobster, but it's really a crayfish," explains Ranger Isabel. The claws are used to catch and hold their prey, but they can't bite you."

"Ranger Isabel," Gabriella raises her hand. "Since the glades are really a river 100 miles long, 40 miles wide and only a foot deep, and there are all these canals and levees and stuff stopping the river, what's going to happen?"

"That's not an easy question," Ranger Isabel answers, "but it could soon be getting better. Since the canals and levees were an attempt to drain the glades, the trick now is to try to get the water flow back as close to normal as we can, because the

whole Everglades ecosystem is fragile and easily disrupted. "Man, that's almost impossible, isn't it?" Esteban frowns.

"Almost, but not quite! There's a huge restoration project under way to take out many of the unnatural barriers clogging up this river of grass. It'll take years to finish, but it will benefit the people and the wildlife of South Florida.

"Listen up," says Maria. She thumbs through her notebook. "We've seen 24 kinds of birds, 4 deer, 2 snakes, and 3 alligators today! Think of how much we could see when this project to save the glades is done!" The class is silent for a moment . . . "Crikey!"

Do you know where your drinking water comes from?

The essence of the Everglades is water. Some parks bring people and water together . . .

The Big Picture . . . Soaring Kites

If you ate only one type of food, would life be simple or difficult? What if that food became harder and harder to find? Consider the endangered snail kite, a raptor living in the Everglades. It eats only apple snails found in south Florida wetlands. Over half of the wetlands have been drained and diverted for farming and development. Will restoration come in time to help the snail kite? Get the facts at www.evergladesplan.org.

The deep blue of the waves dissolve into white foamy water all along the beach at Cape Hatteras National Seashore. With a bright sun and clear skies, it is a perfect day for Richie and Brad to boogie board in the surf while their parents relax on the sand. Other people are swimming, wading or surfing along this stretch of beach. A set of bigger waves crashes ashore. Richie and Brad whoop with laughter at the drenching they receive. After the third wave, a movement farther out in the water catches David's eye.

"Hey, what's that?!" "What's what?" "Over there!" Brad points, "It's a guy in the water waving his arms! See?"

A strong undertow is pulling a man out to sea. He waves frantically.

"Brad! Stay here on the beach and watch him! I'm going for a lifeguard!" Richie sprints down the beach, while Brad doesn't let the man out of his sight. Moments later, two ranger lifeguards run to where Brad is standing. "Right out there!" Brad points.

The rangers hit the water with rescue boards, paddled hard, and soon have the man back on the beach, coughing and scared, but alive. "These kids saved your life, sir," says the ranger named Jenny. The man looks at Brad and Richie. "You two are my heroes," he says.

The boys are a little embarrassed, but very proud. As their parents gather around them at the lifeguard station, Ranger Jenny says, "Hold on, I have something for you." She ducks into the office and comes back out with two badges. "Here," she says, "you two earned junior ranger badges!"

"Sweet!" "Excellent, dude!"

The ocean off Cape Hatteras is home to predators large and small like sharks. Other parks have large predators too. . . . .

The Big Picture . . .

Ninja Turtles

Beautiful, graceful loggerheads are a threatened species of sea turtle that lay their eggs on sandy beaches along the southeast United States. Artificial light, habitat loss, beach erosion, dogs and people can all disturb the sensitive hatchlings.

Find out how you can help at www.nps.gov/caha/seaturt or www.turtles.org.

When Leon and his family arrive at Avalanche Campground in Glacier National Park on a Saturday afternoon, they could tell that someone had been there before them. There is a bag of trash under the picnic table, bottles and cans in the fire pit, and food wrappers scattered around. Before setting up camp, Leon and his sister, Laticia pick up the wrappers, while his grandparents clean the fire pit.

Leon asks his grandfather, "What's wrong with these people, don't they know all this trash can attract bears?!"

Granddad turns as his eye catches some movement in the trees across the meadow. He shouts, "I think it already has!" as a large grizzly bear began to lumber in their direction!

The Big Picture . . .

School for bears?

Problem bears are habituated to human food and garbage. Rangers use aversive conditioning to teach bears to avoid certain areas, like campground and garbage dumps. Methods include rubber bullets and firecracker shotgun shells to scare them away, also relocation and radio collaring. Unfortunately, these are often ineffective, which means problem bears are sometimes killed.

Learn what you can do to help bears at www.nps.gov/glac or www.grizzlydiscoverycenter.com.

CRACK! The sound came whistling through the air. Then, woof! Woof! Bark!

Before Leon had time to scream, the bear ran back into the forest.

"Folks, slowly move back to your camper! Do not run!" a voice, shouts from the road as CRACK! another rubber bullet whizzes toward the bear.

While two rangers and four dogs chase the bear into the woods, another ranger stops to talk to Leon and his family. "Whoever was here before us left trash all over the place!" says Leon excitedly. "How did you know the bear was here?! Were those real bullets?! What kind of dogs are those?!"

"Whoa, slow down," smiles the ranger. "This is a problem bear that has been around the campground getting into trouble. We were out looking for him. We're trying to recondition him, so he doesn't feel welcome in the campground. The bear dogs and rubber bullets are some of the tools we use to discourage him from coming around people."

"What happens if he doesn't learn?" asks Leon.

"He may have to be trapped and relocated or possibly put down if he doesn't change his ways. That's why it's so important to keep and leave a clean camp. Bears need to eat wild food. Grizzlies are already endangered. By cleaning up your camp, you are helping to save that bear's life!"

Can you think of ways to coexist with wildlife where you live?

Dogs aren't the only animals that help rangers perform their duties . . .

The Big Picture . . .

Bear Shepherding?

Some parks are using an innovative tool with four legs for bear management. Karelian bear dogs and their handlers are specially trained to "school" problem bears and help them learn to act like a wild bear again. The result is fewer bear deaths. These hard working dogs have a special purpose in life and are not pets!

Find out more about Karelian bear dogs at **www.beardogs.org**.

"Hey, wait up!" Joey scrambles up the trail. The big kids are getting ahead again. "You better keep up," says Dana, the middle of the three kids. "You don't want a mountain lion to catch you!" "I know what to do if we see a mountain lion. I was listening to the ranger at the visitor center, unlike *some* people I know . . ."

The Walker family is hiking the Harden Lake Trail in Yosemite National Park from their campsite at White Wolf Campground. Evan and Dana lead the way with Mom, while Joey and Dad bring up the rear.

"You know mountain lions are big up here, right?" teases Evan. "Can't scare me," shrugs Joey. "Hey, what's that noise?" asks Dana. "I said, you can't scare . . . " A loud snap came from around a bend in the trail as something crashes through the brush. The Walkers all see something big, brown and moving quickly through the sequoia forest. Dana stammers, "Oh no! It's a . . ."

"It's a ranger!" yells Joey, "on a horse, cool!" A ranger on a dark brown horse rode down the trail. "Hi she says, I'm Ranger Jess, and this is my partner, Thunder." The family gathers around the big stallion. They bury Ranger Jess in an avalanche of questions.

"Whoa, hold on," smiles the ranger. "We use horses for a lot of reasons—we can cover more ground, carry extra gear, have better visibility, and it ties in with the tradition of horse patrols done by the early park rangers."

"What do you do on patrol?" "A lot of what I'm doing right now, talking to folks. I also check on campsites and food storage to keep bears out of trouble. Sometimes I rescue people or give them first aid, sometimes I have to write a ticket, but you know what the best part is?" *"What?"* cried a chorus of voices.

"Taking care of old Thunder, here. Have a good hike!" Ranger Jess rode into the sunset. . . .

In many parks the first rangers used horses to patrol, and some still use them today. There are other animals that help rangers on their patrols.

The Big Picture . . .

Giants from the past

Giant sequoias are amazing trees. Not only are they some of the oldest living things on earth–up to 3,000 years old; they can grow up to 300 feet tall and the largest weighs 12 million pounds. Their 3-inch cones are a prominent symbol for the National Park Service. Ask a park ranger, you'll see it displayed on the uniform hat and belt!

Learn more at www.nps.gov/yose.

"Whoa, that sun is bright!"

It is the end of March during spring break. Janet and her family are on a backcountry ski trip in Denali National Park and Preserve, Alaska. Her cousin Marita is with her too, visiting from Arizona.

"I thought Alaska was dark in the winter," Marita says as she puts on her sunglasses. "Ha! March isn't winter!" exclaims Janet, "It's spring! And spring means lots of sunshine. We gain over seven minutes of light a day now until summer solstice."

"That's why it's so warm." Marita reads the thermometer on her zipper. "My thermometer says 40 degrees Fahrenheit, but it feels like 80 with the sun reflecting off the snow."

The girls and Janet's parents are stopped on a hill for lunch with a great view of Mt. McKinley which is also know as Denali, a Native Alaskan word meaning "The High One". At 20,320 feet, Denali is the highest peak in North America.

"Hey, what's that?" asks Marita. Down the trail in the distance, two indistinct shapes were snaking their way up the hill. Janet takes out her binoculars. "Hey, check it out, it's two dog teams!"

"No way!" Marita had never seen a dog team and is excited. "Sure is, here they come!"

The Big Picture . . .

Denali, crown jewel

What will Denali look like 20, 30 or even 100 years from now? Will wolves howl and caribou roam the rolling tundra and taiga? Hopefully, but it will take more than hope for Denali to remain a crown jewel of the National Park Service.

Learn more about the ecosystem of Denali at www.nps.gov/dena.

From a distance, the dogs, sled and driver appear as one; but as they draw closer, Janet can make out nine hard working huskies and a musher, all moving gracefully over the frozen tundra. A second team of nine strong sled dogs follow, also pulling a sled and musher.

"Whoa, Big Boy, whoa!" the dog driver calls out. The big, black and white lead dog stop right next to the family as the musher sets a snow hook into the trail. "Good dogs! Way to go Big Boy!" He pats all the dogs as he comes up to the front of the team. The happy dogs wag their tails and roll in the snow.

"Hi," says the musher, "I'm Ranger Zach, and this is Ranger Carol. And this," he scratches behind the ears of his lead dog, "is Big Boy."

Growing up in Fairbanks, Alaska, Janet had seen many dog teams, but to Marita, it seems like a dream. "This is so cool! What are you doing out here?" "This is a special trip," says Ranger Carol. "Every year golden eagles return here in February and March to nest. I am an ornithologist. We've been out for a week observing nesting sites."

"Why don't you use a snowmobile? Isn't it quicker?" asks Marita. "I know, I know!" says Janet. "The wilderness of Denali is one of the few places in Alaska where snow-mobiles aren't allowed, right?"

"Right," replies Ranger Zach, "There's no motorized vehicles allowed in the wilderness area of the park, so we use dog power and you're using people power. Part of my job, as a backcountry ranger is to put trail in for visitors. In fact, you're skiing on trail we put in! And if you want to ride a snowmobile, you can do it outside the park wilderness."

Big Boy barks and looks at Ranger Zach. "Well, it looks like Big Boy is ready to go. You know, March is my favorite month in Denali. Enjoy the park!" To Big Boy he says, "OK, let's go!" The two dog teams head east, toward park headquarters.

Can you think of some advantages of traveling by dog team instead of by snowmobile?

Why wait until you are a grown-up to get involved in our parks? Kids can help out too! Turn the page to find out how!

The Big Picture

Denali, crown jewel, part 2

As more people visit Denali, pressure for more roads, increased air traffic, snowmobiles in **wilderness areas** and a proposed railroad are examples of **critical issues** facing park management. It will take careful planning to properly manage Denali National Park and Preserve, while conserving the wilderness and providing for **access**.

Get involved in the issues at **www.denalicitizens.org**.

Rangers

History of Rangers and the National Park Service

From the creation of our first National Park, Yellowstone, in 1872, the parks have been the place where people and their natural and cultural heritage meet. A group of dedicated people help conserve the resources and bring the public—*YOU!*—closer to the parks.

Did you know the first park rangers were soldiers? The uniform that rangers wear today is modified from a soldiers' uniform, including the famous broad rimmed hat. Yellowstone became our first national park in 1872, but The Organic Act, which created the National Park Service, was not written until 1916. The military acted as caretakers until the park service took over. Since the creation of Yellowstone, America's national parks have grown to the almost 400 that we have today!

The Organic Act

This law empowered the **National Park Service** and its rangers to manage the nation's parks. It said that the **National Park Service** *" . . . shall promote and regulate the use of the . . . national parks . . . which purpose is to conserve the scenery and the natural and historic objects and the wildlife therein and to provide for the enjoyment of the same in such manner and by such means as will leave them unimpaired for the enjoyment of future generations . . ."*

In other words, The Organic Act does two things:

1) Protects the things that visitors expect to see at national parks, such as beautiful scenery, lots of wildlife, historic places. The National Park Service does this by conducting scientific research and enforcing rules to minimize the impact we humans have on our parks.

2) Provides good service so visitors can enjoy the parks. The National Park Service does this mainly through the park rangers. The rangers lead hikes, give presentations, answer questions, and give permits. The National Park Service provides public transportation to access parks, as well as other visitor facilities such as museums - all for our enjoyment!

Where Else Do Rangers Work?

Besides national parks, rangers work in many different kinds of areas managed by the National Park Service including national historic sites, national seashores, national battlefields, etc. Other federal government agencies also employ national park rangers to manage their public lands. The National Forest Service and the U.S. Fish and Wildlife Service manage other national public lands. Many state, county and municipal parks throughout the country employ their own rangers.

Work in America's parks

There are a lot of great jobs in the National Park Service. The people who work at these jobs are a diverse group with many different talents. They have one thing in common: they love the parks! A good way to join the National Park Service team is to work as a Volunteer in the Park (VIP), Student Conservation Corps (SCA) member, or Youth Conservation Corps (YCC) volunteer to get some valuable experience. Most jobs in the National Park Service require a degree from a college or university. Biology, resource management, recreation planning, and criminal justice are just a few examples of degrees that rangers can have.

Many rangers start working at smaller parks to gain experience, as competition for jobs in larger, well-known parks is strong. Though lesser known, the smaller urban and rural parks are just as much fun and as important, offering a chance to learn while beginning your career as a park ranger.

Most rangers enjoy several years in one place before applying to another incredible park. Alaska, the U.S. Virgin Islands, Hawaii, and everything in between is waiting to be explored in a career with the National Park Service!

Plot your course at www.nps.gov/personnel/rangers.

Seasonal Park Rangers

Seasonal park rangers have long been the backbone of the National Park Service. Typically hired for one season (summer or winter), these dedicated temporary employees perform every duty imaginable, from maintenance to law enforcement, minus the benefit package of full time government employees. Competition for these jobs is high, as many seasonals return to the same position year after year. Some seasonals use their experience to gain full time, year round, positions.

Find out how to become a seasonal park ranger at www.sep.nps.gov.

Full Time Rangers

The National Park Service hires full time rangers for permanent positions. The dedicated rangers find their careers to be very rewarding as they work in some of the most beautiful and interesting areas of the country. They perform important, meaningful work in an environment that they love.

If a ranger progresses into a management position, he or she may be able to affect the future direction of the national parks.

Volunteer Opportunities

Whether it is a national, state or local municipal park, you can contact the park directly to find out about volunteer opportunities. Ask for the park's volunteer coordinator.

Volunteers in Parks or VIPs
Backcountry patrols, naturalist programs, search and rescue, wildlife study, campground hosting: you name it, volunteers do it! Every year thousands of people volunteer their time to help the National Park Service manage the country's most outstanding resources. Each park administers its own volunteer program, but they all have one thing in common: volunteers are Very Important People!

   Visit www.nps.gov/volunteer.

Student Conservation Association or SCAs
Though you don't need to be a student to be part of the SCA, many are. SCAs work in all aspects of park management, gaining invaluable knowledge in the field, while earning college credit. It's an awesome opportunity to learn while working in the country's best parks.

   Contact: www.thesca.org.

Youth Conservation Corps or YCC
The YCC is a work program for 15 to 18 year olds administered by the National Park Service, the National Forest Service and the U.S. Fish and Wildlife Service. The young men and women of YCC learn valuable life skills while exploring opportunities for careers in conservation. The eight-week projects are a great way to learn about the parks, life, and responsibility while working in some of the most awesome places in the country!

   Get involved at www.fs.fed.us/people/programs/ycc.

Junior Ranger Programs
Junior Rangers are kids who love our parks so much that they're willing to learn all they can about caring for them. Each park has its own Junior Ranger program—some are even on the web! The best part is, once you complete a Junior Ranger program, you get a cool looking Junior Ranger badge to show your friends how much you care about America's parks!

   Check it out at www.nps.gov/webrangers.

What can you do?

Kid Conservation tips:

1) *Learn* how you can help America's parks. Tell your friends.
2) *Take action* to conserve our natural resources.
3) Get out and *enjoy* a park near you!

Kids can make a difference!

Man and the Biosphere

The United Nations Man and the Biosphere program has three special designations for areas that are important internationally.

Biosphere Reserves

Do you think humans are part of nature? How should man interact with the natural world? There are special places in the world where man and nature are in balance and are ideal models of humans interacting with the biosphere. The United Nations calls these special places biosphere reserves.

To be declared a biosphere reserve, the special place must:

1. Be large enough to conserve a diversity of plants, animals and outstanding landscapes.

2. Be a model example of ecologically sustainable development.

3. Provide environmental education and conduct ongoing research of conservation issues.

There are now 218 biosphere reserves in 30 countries. We are fortunate to have 47 in the United States. How many can you find in Ranger Trails?

World Heritage Sites

World Heritage Sites are recognized for having outstanding cultural value to the world. There are 20 in the U.S.

Wetland of International Significance

This denotes a wetland of such importance that its health and viability is significant to more than one country. The Everglades National Park is the only park in the U.S. with this designation.

For more information on the Man and the Biosphere program and a complete list of these special areas worldwide, log onto www.unesco.org

Ranger Skills

Are *you* ready to protect America's parks? Take the ranger skills challenge and test your outdoor knowledge. You'll be ready for your next adventure!

1. You are camping with your family. A small deer enters your campsite and is curiously sniffing the air. It is unafraid and approaches you. Circle the correct response:
   A. You feed it an apple and some cheerios.
   B. You try to pet it.
   C. You don't approach it and try to scare it away by clapping and shouting.
   D. You stand quietly and let it approach you.

2. Fill in the blanks to complete this sentence: Pack ____ ____ pack ____ ____.

3. Keep and leave a clean camp. Animals are attracted to odors from which of the following items:
   A. Dish soap
   B. Crackers
   C. Deodorant and shampoo
   D. Juice
   E. Toothpaste
   F. All of the above

4. You are camping in bear country. Where is a safe place to store your food and toiletries? Circle all correct:
   A. Cooler on the picnic table
   B. Car trunk
   C. Tree
   D. Tent
   E. Food storage locker
   F. Bear resistant food container

5. You can make a campfire any place you want in a national park. True or False?

6. If you become stranded in the backcountry, someone will immediately come to your rescue. True or False?

7. You are hiking on public land and find an artifact. Your friends tell you to keep it. Is this ok? Yes or No?

8. You are hiking in a desert park. You want to go farther but your water bottle is almost empty. Should you take a chance that you will find a water source? Yes or No?

9. Is it a good idea to snack and drink frequently when hiking? Yes or No?

10. What type of footwear is appropriate for walking in the wilderness?
    A. Sneakers
    B. Sandals
    C. Soccer shoes
    D. Dress shoes
    E. Hiking Boots

11. List some ideas of safety gear you would carry with you on a day hike:

12. You are visiting a national park and want to hike in the backcountry but are unsure what to expect. Whom should you ask for advice on how to prepare?

Answers:
1) C. 2) Pack it in, pack it out. 3) F. 4) B, E, F. 5) False. 6) False. 7) No. 8) No.
9) Yes. 10) E. 11) Map and compass, full water bottle, snacks, raingear, a grownup. 12) A park ranger.

How did you score?

9 to 12: Congratulations, you have excellent ranger skills! You are now ready to protect and enjoy America's parks!

6 to 8: Your skills are good, but study more before you go on your next adventure.

5 or less: You really need to get out more!

Most of these questions just take a little sensible thinking on your part – you must consider the results of your actions while visiting the parks. You can learn more about how to protect America's parks from a ranger next time you visit a park.

Word Scrambles   Clues

1. OLANANIT KRSAP   The best idea America ever had.
2. ATLRNUA RSCEUSORE   Treasures of the earth.
3. GIRAONC TCA   It created the National Park Service.
4. RKAP GRAERN   Person working in our parks.
5. OSITVISR   People who enjoy our parks.
6. VSNCIORONEAT   Mission of the National Park Service.
7. WLELEYOTOSN   Our first national park.
8. SEWDELNIRS   The backcountry.
9. GANDERENED SCEIPSE   Animals almost gone.
10. TABIHAT   An animal's home.
11. TEAHGREI   Our cultural legacy.
12. TDEEARVUN   Having a great time.

Answers:
1) national parks 2) natural resources 3) The Organic Act 4) park ranger
5) visitors 6) conservation 7) Yellowstone 8) wilderness 9) endangered species
10) habitat 11) heritage 12) adventure

Exploring America's parks on the Web

Look for these symbols in front of the web site, it means that the site is *especially good* for:

K Kids   **P** Parents   **T** Teachers

Air Quality

www.propanevehicle.org
K   www.nps.gov/transportation
K   www.nature.nps.gov
T, K   www.epa.gov/airnow
www.itsa.org (Intelligent transportation)

Alaska Issues

www.trustees.org (Trustees for Alaska)
www.alaskacoalition.org
P, T   www.northern.org (Northern Alaska Environmental Center)

Alpine Environment

www.eurac.edu/org/alpineenvironment

Anasazi Culture

T, K   http://sipapu.gsu.edu
www.nps.gov/chcu (Chaco Culture NHP)
www.nps.gov/hove (Hovenweep NM)
www.nps.gov/nabr (Natural Bridges NM)
www.nps.gov/wupa (Wupatki NM)
www.nps.gov/nava (Navajo NM)
www.nps.gov/moca (Montezuma's Castle NM)
www.nps.gov/cach (Canyon de Chelly NM)
www.nps.gov/azru (Aztec Ruins NM)

Archeology

T, K   www.cr.nps.gov (NPS links to the past)
www.saa.org (Society, American Archeology)
www.swanet.org (SW Archeology)
T   www.nationaltrust.org (Historic Preservation)

Bears

K   www.bear.org (North American Bear Center)
T, K   www.bearbiology.com (International Association Bear Management. and Research)
K   www.grizzlydiscoveryctr.com
www.mountainnature.com/wildlife/bears (Bear safety tips)
www.usparks.about.com click on best state parks, search for bear safety tips
www.mountain-prairie.fws.gov (US Fish & Wildlife Service)
T, K   www.beardogs.org (bear shepherding)

Biosphere Reserves

T   www.unesco.org/mab (UN, Man and Biology Program)
T   www.mabnetamericas.org (Biosphere Reserves, US)

Climate Change/Global Warming

T, K   www.arm.gov (Atmospheric Radiation Measurement)
K, P, T   www.usgcrp.gov (US Global Change Research Program)
T   http://yosemite.epa.gov/oar/globalwarming.nsf
T   www.hdgc.epp.cmu.edu/teachersguide
K   www.onesky.umich.edu click on projects (Kids as global scientists on biodiversity, climate)
T, K   www.epa.gov/globalwarming/kids

Denali NP&P Issues

P   www.denali.org (Elderhostel)
P, T   www.dcc.org (Denali Citizens Council)
P, T   www.denaliinstitute.org

Dinosaurs

T, K   www.search4dinosaurs.com
K, P, T   www.enchantedlearning.com/subjects/dinosaurs
T, K   www.dinosauria.com

50

T, K www.paleoportal.org
T, K www.search.eb.com/dinosaurs

Forest Conservation
T, K www.rainforest-alliance.org
www.forests.org
www.americanforests.org
www.cifor.cgiar.org (Ctr. For Intern. Forestry Research)
www.iwokrama.org (International Rain Forest Conservation)

K Conservation Sites for Kids
www.turner.com/planet (Captain Planet Foundation)
www.kidsagainstpollution.org
www.kidsface.org (Kids for a Clean Environment)
www.ran.org click on rain forest heros (Rainforest Action Net)
www.nwf.org/kids (National Wildlife Fed)

Ocean Conservation
T www.sanctuaries.nos.noaa.gov
T, K www.npca.org/marine_and_coastal/marine_wildlife
K, P, T www.shiftingbaselines.org
K, P, T www.turtles.org
K, P, T www.cccturtle.org (Caribbean Conservation Corps.)
T, K www.orf.org (Ocean Research Foundation)
K, P, T www.seaweb.org

Conservation Organizations-U.S,
www.americansfornationalparks.org
K, P, T www.arcticdance.com (Mardy Murie story)
P, T www.muriecenter.org (Mardy Murie center)
P, T www.hcn.org (Highcountry News)
P www.nwf.org (Nat. Wildlife Fed.)
P www.npca.org (Nat. Parks & Conservation Assn)
P www.defenders.org (Defenders of Wildlife)
P www.sierraclub.org
(P) www.audubon.org
P www.iwla.org (Izaak Walton League)

K, P, T www.railstotrails.org
P www.earthshare.org
P www.nature.org (Nature Conservancy)
P www.wwfus.org (World Wildlife Fund-U.S.)
P www.nrdc.org (Natural Resources Defense Council)

Wetlands Conservation
P www.ducks.org (Ducks Unlimited)
http://users.erols.com/wetlandg (Nat. Wetlands Conservation Alliance)
www.americanbirding.org

Wildlife Conservation-Global
www.wri.org (World Resources Inst.)
www.awf.org (African Wildlife Found.)
T, K www.conservation.org (Conservation Int.)
P www.earthjustice.org (Natural Resources Defense Council)
T, K www.biodiversityhotspots.org (Center. For Applied Biodiversity Science)
T, K http://mbgnet.mobot.org (Biomes)
K, P, T www.worldwildlife.org (World Wildlife Fund)
www.panda.org (World Wildlife Fund)
K www.pbs.org/nature
T, K www.thewildones.org (Wildlife Trust)

Earth Summit 2002
www.earthsummit.info
www.earth-info.net
www.un.org/esa/earthsummit
www.earthsummit2002.org

Environmental Education
T www.nrel.gov/education (renewable energy)
T, K www.idealist.com (Action without Borders)
K www.eduseek.com
T www.eetap.org (Environmental Education Training Partnership)
T, K www.ditc-eef.org (Environmental Ed. Foundation)
K, P, T www.rprogress.org (Redefining Progress)

For a quick link to these sites go to www.rangertrailsadventure.com

T, K   www.urbanext.uiuc.edu/ecosystems
T   www.eelink.net (NA Assn. For Environmental Ed.)
T, K   www.arkive.org
T, K   www.nmfs.noaa.gov/prot_res (Nat. Marine Fisheries Protected Resources)
T   www.nps.gov/learn
T, K   www.nps.gov/akso/education (Ed. Materials, Alaska)
T   www.eduweb.com (Educational Web Adventures)

Environmental News
K, P, T   www.earthwatch.unep.net (UN Systemwide Earthwatch)
www.environment.about.com (Environmental Issues)
http://news.fws.gov (U.S. Fish & Wildlife Svc.)
http://news.nationalgeographic.com
www.enn.com (Environ. News Network)
www.nps.gov/morningreport (NPS Ranger Morning Report)

Everglades
K, P, T   www.evergladesplan.org
www.floridaconservation.org
www.sofia.usgs.gov (U.S. Geologic Survey)
www.floridafisheries.com
P, T   www.sfwmd.gov (South Florida Water Management District)

Fire Ecology
T   www.fire-ecology.org
T, K   www.nps.gov/fire
T   www.nps.gov/fire/ecology
T   www.ttrs.org (Tall Timbers Research Station)
T, K   www.blm.gov/education

Government Agencies
www.arm.gov (Atmospheric Radiation Measurement)
www.earthobservatory.nasa.gov (Climate Change)
www.epa.gov/airnow (Air Quality Index)
www.nps.gov (Nat. Park Service)
www.epa.gov (Environmental Protection Agency)
www.fws.gov (Fish & Wildlife Svc.)
www.blm.gov (Bureau of Land Mgmt.)
www.fs.fed.us (Nat. Forest Svc.)
www.state.gov/g/oes (Bureau of Oceans & Environment and Scientific Affairs)
www.usace.army.mil (Army Corps of Engineers)
www.nmfs.noaa.gov (Nat. Marine Fisheries Svc.)
www.doi.gov (Dept. of Interior)
www.em.doe.gov (Dept. of Energy, Office Environ. Mgmt)
www.serc.si.edu (Smithsonian Environ. Research Center.)
www.usbr.gov (Bureau of Reclamation)
www.doi.gov.bureauindian-affairs.gov (Bureau of Indian Affairs
www.mms.gov (Minerals Management Service
www.osmre.gov (Office of Surface Mining)
www.usgs.gov (U.S. Geological Survey)
www.usgcrp.gov (U.S. Global Change Research Program)
www.nrel.gov (National Renewable Energy Laboratory)
www.nsf.gov (National Science Foundation)
www.arm.gov (Atmospheric Radiation Measurement)

Government Sites for Kids
www.nps.gov/webrangers (Junior Rangers on the Web)
www.epa.gov/kids (Environmental Protection Agency)
www.blm.gov/education (Bureau of Land Management)
www.bensguide.gpo.gov (Links to all government agencies with kid sites)
www.eere.energy.gov/kids (Dept. of Energy)
www.epa.gov/safewater/kids
www.fws.gov/endangered (Endangered Species)
www.doi.gov/kids (Dept. of Interior)
www.nps.gov/learn

www.mms.gov/mmskids **(Minerals Management Service)**
www.usgs.gov/education **(U.S. Geologic Survey)**
http://earthquake.usgs.gov/4kids
http://terraweb.wr.usgs.gov/kids
http://astrogeology.usgs.gov/kids
www.epa.gov/recyclecity
www.fs.fed.us/spf/woodsy **(Forest Service)**
www.americaslibrary.gov/cgi-bin/page.cgi **(Library of Congress)**
www.fs.fed.us/outdoors/naturewatch
www.geo.nsf.gov **(National Science Found.)**
www.epa.gov/globalwarming/kids
http://ga.water.usgs.gov/edu **(Ground Water)**

Invasive Species
www.hear.org **(Hawaiian Ecosystems at Risk Project)**
www.invasive.org

National Parks Profiled in Ranger Trails
www.nps.gov/grca **(Grand Canyon NP)**
www.nps.gov/dino **(Dinosaur NM)**
www.nps.gov/meve **(Mesa Verde NP)**
www.nps.gov/inde **(Independence NHP)**
www.nps.gov/havo **(Hawaii Volcanoes NP)**
www.nps.gov/crla **(Crater Lake NP)**
www.nps.gov/mora **(Mt. Rainier NP)**
www.nps.gov/acad **(Acadia NP)**
www.nps.gov/gaar **(Gates of the Arctic NP&P)**
www.nps.gov/yell **(Yellowstone NP)**
www.nps.gov/ever **(Everglades NP)**
www.nps.gov/caha **(Cape Hatteras NS)**
www.nps.gov/glac **(Glacier NP)**
www.nps.gov/yose **(Yosemite NP)**
www.nps.gov/dena **(Denali NP&P)**
www.nps.gov/glca **(Glen Canyon NRA)**
www.usbr.gov/lc/hooverdam

Visitor Information-National Parks
T, K   www.nationalparks.org
K, P, T   www.us-national-parks.net
P   www.americansouthwest.net
P   www.llbean.com/parksearch
P   www.sidecanyon.com
P   www.usparks.about.com

Outdoor Skills
www.nols.edu **(National Outdoor Leadership School)**
K, P, T   www.Lnt.org **(Leave no Trace Principles)**
www.outwardbound.com

Ranger Career Information
www.anpr.org **(Association National Park Rangers)**
www.nps.gov/personnel **click on rangers**
www.sep.nps.gov **(Seasonal Park Rangers)**
www.nps.gov/volunteer **(VIPs)**
www.thesca.org **(Student Conservation Assn.)**
www.fs.fed.us/people/volunteer/ycc **(Youth Conservation Corps)**
www.eco.org **(Environmental Careers Org.)**
www.jobmonkey.com/parks
www.angelfire.com/mo/parkranger

Raptors
T, K   www.buteo.com
T, K   www.birds-of-prey.org
T   www.nbpc.co.uk
P, T   www.peregrinefund.org
K, P, T   www.hawkmountain.org

River Ecosystems
T   www.water-ed.org
T   www.americanrivers.org
P, T   www.glencanyon.org

RS2477 Issues
T   www.suwa.org **(Southern Utah Wilderness Alliance)**
T   www.rs2477.com **(Highway Robbery Coalition)**

Natural Science
T, K   www.earthsky.com **(Science, astronomy education**
T   www.exploratorium.edu **(Science museum)**

For a quick link to these sites go to www.rangertrailsadventure.com

T, K   www.earthobservatory.nasa.gov
T, K   www.greenfacts.org
T, K   www.studyworksonline.com
T   www.nsta.org (National Science Teachers)
T   www.education.noaa.gov
T   www.learner.org (Professional teacher development)
(K)(P)   www.redjellyfish.com (Environmentally responsible shopping)
T, K   www.scienceblog.com
K   www.riverdeep.net (Kids natural sciences)
K, P, T   www.kidinfo.com (Educational reference resource)
T   www.enc.org (K-12 math & science teacher)
T   www.nas.edu (Nat. Academy of Sciences)
T, K   www.ucsusa.org (Union of Concerned Scientists)
K, P, T   www.bonus.com
K, P, T   www.encyclopedia.com
K, P, T   www.myreportlinks.com

Subsistence
T   www.arctic-council.org
T   www.nativeknowledge.org

Sustainable Development
T   www.iucn.org (livelihoods and landscapes)
P, T   www.heifer.org (Heifer Int.)
P, T   www.worldlandtrust.org

U.S. History, Revolutionary War
K, P, T   www.ushistory.org
K, P, T   www.fieldtrip.com
T   www.school.discovery.com/lessonplans
K, P, T   www.timeplace.org
K, P, T   www.revwar.com
K, P, T   www.cr.nps.gov/seac/links3 (Archeology & History links)

K, P, T   www.americanhistory.si.edu/notkid/index
T, K   www.cpluhna.edu (Land use history-Col. Plateau)

Volcanoes
T, K   http://volcano.und.nodak.edu
T, K   www.volcanoes.com
T, K   www.geology.sdsu.edu/how_volcanoes_work

Water Quality
T, K   http://.ga.water.usgs.gov/edu
K, P, T   www.groundwater.org

Wilderness Issues
T   www.leopold.wilderness.net (Scientific leadership to sustain wilderness.)
P   www.action.leaveitwild.org (Campaign for America's Wilderness)
P   www.wilderness.org (Wilderness Society)
www.ourcolorado.org (Colorado Environmental Coal.)

Wolves
P, T   www.predatorconservation.org
T   http://endangered.fws.gov

World Heritage Sites-U.S.
T   www.cr.npa.gov/heritage/areas

Yellowstone Coalition
www.greateryellowstone.org

Yosemite
www.nps.gov/yose/news/graphics
www.yni.org (Yosemite Institute)

Glossary

These abbreviations are used throughout the Glossary:
- NHP: National Historic Park
- NM: National Monument
- NP: National Park
- NP&P: National Park and Preserve
- NS: National Seashore

Access. The right to reach, use or visit public land. *Denali NP&P, Rangers.*

Alpine. The part of a mountain above treeline. *Mt. Rainier NP.*

Alluvium. Sediment transported and deposited by flowing water. *Grand Canyon NP.*

Alternative Transportation System. Transportation powered with energy derived from sources other than petroleum. *Acadia NP.*

Anasazi culture. A prehistoric North American people native to the southwestern U. S. *Mesa Verde NP.*

Archeologist. A scientist who studies ancient cultures through the excavation and analysis of remains. *Mesa Verde NP.*

Arctic. The far north, close to the North Pole and above the Arctic Circle. *Gates of the Arctic NP.*

ARPA (Archeological Resources Protection Act). The federal law which protects cultural resources on public lands. *Mesa Verde NP.*

Artifact. An object made by earlier humans. *Mesa Verde NP.*

Aversive conditioning. Retraining a wild animal, such as a bear, to avoid certain areas or behaviors through negative reinforcement. *Glacier NP.*

Backcountry. The less easily reached part of a park. The wilderness. *Denali NP&P.*

Biologist. A scientist who studies living organisms. *Gates of the Arctic NP&P.*

Biome. A major ecological community of organisms, occupying a large area, (i.e., tropical rain forest). *Web Sites.*

Biosphere. The part of the earth and its atmosphere in which organisms live. *Introduction, Man and the Biosphere.*

Canus lupus. The scientific name for the gray wolf. *Yellowstone NP.*

Carabiner. A piece of climbing gear made of aluminum, used to link other pieces of equipment. *Mt. Rainier NP.*

Climate. Prevailing weather conditions for a particular region. *Gates of the Arctic NP&P.*

Coexist. To exist in mutual tolerance. *Glacier NP.*

Conservation. Preservation of the natural environment. *Volunteers, Man & the Biosphere, Web Sites.*

Crampons. Short metal spikes that attach to boots, used by mountain climbers for traction on ice. *Mt. Rainier NP.*

Critical issues. The most important issues that pose threats to the conservation of an area. *Meet the Rangers, Denali NP&P.*

Delist. The process of taking an animal or plant off the endangered species list by the US Fish and Wildlife Service. *Yellowstone NP.*

Delta. The accumulation of sediment at the mouth of a river, where it flows into the sea or a lake. *Grand Canyon NP.*

Divert. To change the course of water flow from a river so it can be used by people, or to prevent flooding. An example would be a dam. *Everglades NP, Grand Canyon NP.*

Ecology. The study of the relations of organisms to one another and to their physical surroundings. *Crater Lake NP, Grand Canyon NP.*

Ecosystem. A biological community of interacting organisms and their physical environment. *Denali NP&P, Everglades NP, Hawaii Volcanoes NP, Mt. Rainier NP, Yellowstone NP.*

Emissions. Pollutants produced by internal combustion engines. *Acadia NP.*

Endangered species. Plants and animals receiving federal protection due to the threat of extinction. *Meet the Rangers, Everglades NP, Glacier NP, Hawaii Volcanoes NP, Yellowstone N.P.*

Endangered Species Act. A federal law protecting our endangered plants and animals. *Yellowstone NP.*

Erosion. The wearing away of rock, soil, or sand by the processes of water, wind or ice. *Cape Hatteras NS.*

Estuary. The tidal zone at the mouth of a river that provides a nutrient rich environment for marine life. *Grand Canyon NP.*

Exotic species. Non-native species of plants and animals that invade and threaten native species. *Hawaii Volcanoes NP.*

Fireline. A wildland firefighting technique that clears vegetation down to mineral soil. *Crater Lake NP.*

Florida panther. A subspecies of the mountain lion that lives only in Florida. *Everglades NP.*

Food storage. Regulations in most parks require food to be in a bear resistant container. *Yosemite NP.*

Fossil. Remains or impression of a plant or animal hardened in rock. *Dinosaur NM, Mesa Verde NP.*

Glacier. A mass of ice on land formed by the accumulation of snow on high ground over centuries. Occurs where winter snowfall exceeds summer melting. *Mt. Rainier NP.*

Habitat. The dwelling place of a species providing a particular set of environmental conditions. *Cape Hatteras NS, Everglades NP, Hawaii Volcanoes NP.*

Habituated. Pertaining to wildlife becoming accustomed or desensitized to human presence or activity. *Glacier NP.*

Heritage. The history of a culture: artifacts, buildings, traditions that have significant cultural value. *Mesa Verde NP.*

Initial assessment. An emergency medical procedure. The first steps taken to discover and deal with life threatening problems. *Acadia NP.*

Liberty. Freedom to do as one pleases. *Independence NHP.*

Meadow. An area of permanent grassland and wildflowers. *Yellowstone NP.*

Mountaineering. Alpine mountain climbing, requiring technical skill. *Mt. Rainier NP.*

Musher. A person who drives and trains a team of sled dogs. *Denali NP&P.*

Naturalist. An expert in natural history. *Volunteering In Our Parks.*

Natural resources. Plants, animals, minerals, water, etc. found in nature that can be used and enjoyed by people. *Gates of the Arctic NP&P.*

Organic Act. The law creating the National Park Service. *History of the Park Service.*

Ornithologist. A scientist who studies birds. *Denali NP&P.*

Paleontologist. A scientist who studies dinosaur fossils. *Dinosaur NM.*

Patrol. Traveling around park land in order to protect and supervise it. *Grand Canyon NP, Mt Rainier NP, Volunteers.*

Predator. A carnivorous animal, that is, an animal that eats meat. *Gates of the Arctic NP&P, Yellowstone NP.*

Prey species. An animal eaten by predators. *Dinosaur NM, Everglades NP, Yellowstone NP.*

Ranger. A person who works at a park performing various duties for the National Park Service.

- **Backcountry.** A ranger who patrols remote areas of a park. *Denali NP&P.*
- **Interpretive.** A ranger who gives presentations, and leads hikes on natural and cultural history. *Independence NHP.*
- **General.** A ranger who gives information at visitor centers and fee booths.
- **Law Enforcement.** A ranger with special training and authority to enforce federal law in the parks. *Acadia NP, Dinosaur NM, Mesa Verde NP.*
- **Lifeguard.** A ranger with special training to perform water rescue in the parks. *Cape Hatteras NS.*
- **Mountaineering.** A ranger who ensures the safety of mountain climbers. *Mt. Rainier NP.*
- **Seasonal.** A ranger hired to work in a park for part of the year, usually when the most visitors are there. *Rangers*

Raptor. A bird of Prey, such as an owl, hawk, falcon, etc. *Everglades NP.*

Recondition. To teach a wild animal, such as a bear, to act wild and avoid seeking human food. *Glacier NP.*

Reintroduction. To place breeding pairs of an endangered species in a specified area in hopes of establishing a sustainable population. *Yellowstone NP.*

Relocation. A bear management technique, which involves capturing a problem bear and releasing it in another area in hopes of avoiding human encounters. *Glacier NP.*

Restoration. A plan that attempts to return a damaged ecosystem to its natural state. *Everglades NP.*

Revolutionist. A person who seeks to overthrow a government, as during the Revolutionary War. *Independence NHP.*

Riparian area. A transition zone bordering a lake, sea, or river. *Grand Canyon NP.*

Scat. Animal excrement. *Yellowstone NP.*

Sign. Clues that show where an animal has been, such as tracks, scat, rub marks, etc. *Yellowstone NP.*

Slough. (rhymes with flew) A side channel of a river that moves slower than the main channel. *Everglades NP.*

Snow hook. A sharp, curved piece of metal, attached to a dog sled, which a musher can stomp into the snow, or hook around a tree to keep a dog team from moving. *Denali NP&P.*

Subsistence lifestyle. How people live in a remote, roadless area, obtaining their food by hunting and gathering. *Gates of the Arctic NP&P.*

Summer solstice. The mid point of summer when the earth is closest to the sun. *Denali NP&P.*

Sustainable development. Using a resource in a responsible way so that it is not depleted. *Man & the Biosphere.*

Sustainable population. A group of animals managed so they can maintain or increase in number. *Denali NP&P.*

Taiga. Forest adjacent to arctic tundra. *Denali NP&P.*

Threatened species. A plant or animal receiving protection under the Endangered Species Act because it is at risk of becoming endangered. *Cape Hatteras NS, Yellowstone NP.*

Treeline. The highest point on a mountainside where trees can grow. *Mt. Rainier NP.*

Tundra. Treeless arctic and alpine regions that may be bare of trees but support mosses, lichens, and dwarf plants. *Denali NP&P.*

Vulcanologist. A scientist who studies volcanoes. *Hawaii Volcanoes NP.*

Wetlands. An area covered permanently, occasionally, or periodically by fresh or salt water. *Everglades NP.*

Wilderness area. Public land which is managed to maintain its natural state where no development or mechanized vehicles are allowed. *Denali NP&P.*

Wildland firefighter. A person trained to fight forest fires. *Crater Lake NP.*

Suggested Reading

Exciting true stories have been written by former and current park rangers. These books make research on the life of a park ranger very entertaining. Here's a sampling:

A Woman in the Great Outdoors: Adventures in the National Park Service
Melody Webb
University of New Mexico Press 2003

Park Rangers: True Stories from a Ranger's Career in America's National Parks
Nancy Eileen Muleady-Meacham
Vishnu Temple Press 2004

National Park Ranger: An American Icon
Charles R. Farabee
Roberts Rhinehart Publishers 2003

Take Down Flag and Feed Horses
Bill Everhart
University of Illinois Press 1998

Ex-rangers have written action-packed novels based on their experience. Check out this series:

The Anna Pigeon Series
Nevada Barr, a former actress and ranger writes mysteries set in the wilderness.
Various publishers

Some children's books give a nice introduction to what it means to be a ranger:

Exploring Parks with Ranger Dockett
Alice K. Flanagan
Children's Press 1998

Park Rangers: Focus, Careers
Meredith Costain
Rebound by Sagebrush 2001

Another ex-ranger has created an inspirational and beautiful book showing how remarkable feats by dedicated people can make a difference:

The Making of the National Parks: An American Idea
Kim Heacox
National Geographic 2004

Authors Jeff and Lori Yanuchi have over twenty-one seasons experience as national park rangers between them. Jeff had worked as a seasonal park ranger for fifteen years in seven different parks. Lori worked as a ranger with the sled dogs at Denali National Park for six years.

With twin sons Stony and BJ, and thirty hard working Alaskan huskies, Lori and Jeff operate Denali Dog Freight Expeditions. Their unique business delivers mountain climbing gear by dog team for the climbers attempting the north side of Mt. McKinley.

"The Canine Sherpas of Mt. McKinley" are the product of Jeff and Lori's passion for sled dogs. They developed their own kennel of freighting dogs specifically suited for mushing in the extreme conditions of the Alaska Range.

Lori has also written *Running with the Big Dogs: A Sled Dog Puppy Grows Up in Denali National Park, Alaska*

Visit Lori and Jeff at www.denalidogfreight.com

Illustrator James R. Morris is an award winning artist specializing in Alaskan nature and aviation. He has created numerous stunning and intricate commissioned aviation pieces, mainly for the United States Air Force. Jim is well known for his Alaskan comical drawings.

Jim's collectible art is drawn in pen and ink, and enhanced with airbrush techniques.

As a child in Bremerton, Washington, Jim was inspired by his mother, Judy, a commercial artist. Blessed and self-taught, Jim has been a freelance artist since 1984. Moving to Alaska in 1991 enabled Jim to pursue his artwork while enjoying the beauty and wonders in The Great Land.

Jim enjoys hiking, camping, photography, and building model ships. Jennie, Jim's very supportive wife, thoroughly enjoys promoting his artwork.

"This is the first children's book I have illustrated and I hope that the pictures bring joy to your heart and awake an interest in your mind to investigate America's beautiful parks".

Visit Jim and Jennie at www.sunjamstudios.com

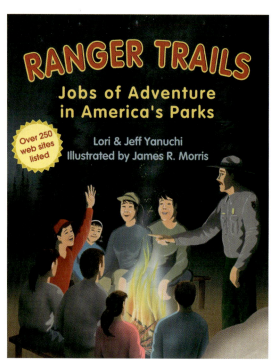

Ranger Trails: Jobs of Adventure in America's Parks

by Lori and Jeff Yanuchi

Children from across our nation meet rangers protecting America's parks. A great reading adventure now and an inspiration for a future career working in America's parks.
64 pages.   ISBN 0-9670177-2-6

Running with the Big Dogs A Sled Dog Puppy Grows Up in Denali National Park, Alaska

by Lori Yanuchi and Wendy Brown

A full color story book that invites children to mush along with the sled dogs of Denali. Share the wonder of a puppy as you follow him through his first year of adventure and learning.
32 pages.   ISBN 0-9670177-0-X

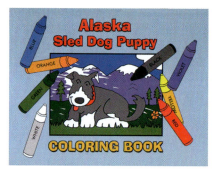

Alaska Sled Dog Puppy Coloring Book

For younger children. Learn about the daily life of a sled dog puppy. Bring the story to life with color.
24 pages.   ISBN 0-9670177-1-8

Order Form

Name:	
Address:	
Phone:	
Credit Card #:	
Expiration Date:	Visa Mastercard Discover AmEx
Signature:	

Ridge Rock Press
P.O. Box 255
Healy, Alaska 99743
fax: 907-683-7737

COUNT	TITLE	PRICE	TOTAL
	Ranger Trails	$12.95	
	Running with the Big Dogs	$ 8.95	
	Alaska Sled Dog Puppy Coloring Book	$ 4.95	
	Shipping	$ 3.50	
	TOTAL